SYMBOLIC
HEAT

SYMBOLIC HEAT

Gender, Health & Worship
among the Tamils of
South India and Sri Lanka

DENNIS B. McGILVRAY

Mapin Publishing Pvt Ltd, Ahmedabad

in association with

University of Colorado Museum, Boulder

Reprinted in 2003
in the United States of America by
Grantha Corporation
80 Cliffedgeway, Middletown, NJ 07701

in association with
University of Colorado Museum
Boulder, CO 80309 USA
and
Mapin Publishing Pvt. Ltd.
31 Somnath Road, Usmanpura
Ahmedabad 380013 INDIA
email: mapin@icenet.net
www.mapinpub.com

Distributed in North America by
Antique Collectors' Club
Market Street Industrial Park
Wappingers' Falls, NY 12590
Tel: 800-252 5321 • Fax: 845-297 0068
email: info@antiquecc.com
www.antiquecc.com

Distributed in the United Kingdom,
Europe & the Middle East by
Art Books International
Unit 14 Groves Business Centre
Shipton Road, Milton-under-Wychwood
Chipping Norton
Oxon OX7 6JP
UK
Tel: 1993 830000 • Fax: 1993 830007
email: sales@art-bks.com
www.artbooksinternational.co.uk

ISBN: 0-944142-87-7 (Grantha)
ISBN: 81-85822-52-2 (Mapin)
LC: 97-75689

Edited by Mallika Sarabhai
Designed by Jatin Banker/
Mapin Design Studio
Printed by Ajanta Offset, New Delhi, India

Jacket Illustrations
Front
A red village goddess displays the marks of her
ambivalent personality.
Back
A small boy carries lunch cannisters to his
mother while she works on repairs to the steps
surrounding the bathing tank at the Meenakshi
Sundaresvarar Temple in Madurai, Tamilnadu.
At this age, children are cherished for their
innocence and purity of heart.

To my Tamil and Muslim friends, who taught me the meaning of warmth

ACKNOWLEDGEMENTS

SYMBOLIC HEAT, Gender, Health, and Worship among the Tamils of South India and Sri Lanka is published in conjunction with a travelling exhibit of the same name produced by the University of Colorado Museum. Funding for the exhibit was provided by:

University of Colorado Museum

Chancellor, University of Colorado at Boulder

Committee on University Scholarly Publications

University of Colorado President's Fund for the Humanities

Department of Anthropology, Boulder campus

Asian Studies Program, Boulder campus

Support for the publication of this book has been provided by the following sources at the University of Colorado at Boulder:

University Museum Publications Fund

Associate Vice Chancellor for Academic Affairs

College of Arts and Sciences Advancement Fund

Dean of the Graduate School

Department of Anthropology

CONTENTS

THE TAMILS

SYMBOLIC HEAT is sacred female energy.

For the Tamil Hindus of south India and Sri Lanka, a concept of physical and spiritual heat as female energy influences their diet, their health practices, their view of men and women, and their worship of the gods.

THE TAMILS

The Tamil people live throughout the southern Indian state of Tamilnadu (population 61 million) and in parts of Sri Lanka (population 18 million). Many Tamils have also settled overseas in Malaysia and Singapore, as well as in Europe, Canada, and the United States.

Tamil belongs to the Dravidian family of languages, possibly the earliest surviving language group in the South Asian subcontinent.

Ancient Tamil *Sangam* poetry records a civilisation well established in South India at the time of Christ. During the medieval period (A.D. 600-1600) the royal patronage of rival dynasties – Chera, Pallava, Chola, Pandya – supported literature, art, and the construction of great Hindu temples. Through both peaceful migrations and military invasions during this period, Tamils also became well established in northern and eastern Sri Lanka.

Today the vast majority of Tamils follow the Hindu religion, but in the medieval period there were also Tamil Buddhists and Jains. There are Tamil-speaking Christians and Muslims as well.

In Sri Lanka (formerly known as Ceylon), the Tamils, who form 18% of the population, and the Sinhalese, who constitute 74%, have shared similar modes of subsistence, kinship patterns, and caste organisation for centuries. Although the Sinhalese are primarily Theravada Buddhists, and the Tamils are predominantly Hindus, linguistic rivalry rather than religious difference has been the most important source of tension in the 20th century. Tamil identity is closely linked to the Tamil language. In the period since Independence in 1948, Tamils and Sinhalese have been increasingly polarised by bitter ethnic violence, exacerbated by feelings of linguistic pride and charges of discrimination in government policies. Tamils complain of restricted access to higher education and professional careers, as well as massive government-sponsored resettlement of Sinhalese farmers in the northeastern region where Tamils and Muslims have historically predominated. When, in the late 1970s, democratic efforts on

The elephant-headed god of beginnings, remover of obstacles, is known by several names. *Ganesha* (Lord of the Hosts), *Vināyakar* (Lord of Wisdom), *Piḷḷaiyār* (The Great Child). Tamils worship him at the outset, before they start something new.

behalf of the Tamils were seen to have failed, a strong guerrilla movement emerged to fight for an independent homeland in the northeast to be called Tamil Eelam. Since then, a diaspora of Sri Lankan Tamil refugees and asylum-seekers has sought safety and a new life in India, Europe, and North America.

The photographs in this collection were taken before the outbreak of armed conflict in 1983. They depict Tamil life in Sri Lanka before destruction and tragic violence engulfed the regular patterns of daily existence in the northern and eastern regions of the island.

TAMILNADU

Blocked by western mountains from receiving all of the southwest monsoon rains, Tamilnadu is rocky and semi-arid, except where irrigation makes wet-rice cultivation possible.

Tamils live primarily in rural farming villages, but urban areas are growing rapidly. The oldest towns in Tamilnadu, such as Madurai, were built around large Hindu temples, while the newer cities such as Madras (Chennai) were laid out by the British.

Irrigated rice fields and coconut trees near Palani, Madurai District, Tamilnadu.

Top
A middle class urban neighbourhood near the foot of the Rock Fort in Tiruchirappalli, Tamilnadu.

Centre
A traditional street in the village of Mudaiyur, near Polur, North Arcot District. The hereditary caste occupation here is stone-carving, and some discarded stone fragments can be seen in front of one of the houses. The molded verandahs flanking each doorway are places for men to relax and entertain guests.

Bottom
A stone-lined irrigation well west of Pudukkottai, Tiruchirappalli District. Using ropes and a pulley, teams of bullocks are used to raise water which then flows into the nearby fields. Some of these large wells have stone inscriptions dating back to the medieval period.

Movie posters in Madras (Chennai) announce popular Tamil films. The Indian motion picture industry is the largest in the world. Titles shown include "Jungle Man" (left), and "A Love Worthy of Devotion" (right). The late Chief Minister of Tamilnadu, Mr. M.G. Ramachandran, was a popular movie star, and cinema personalities and screenwriters continue to figure prominently in Tamilnadu politics.

TAMIL SPEAKING REGIONS OF SOUTH ASIA

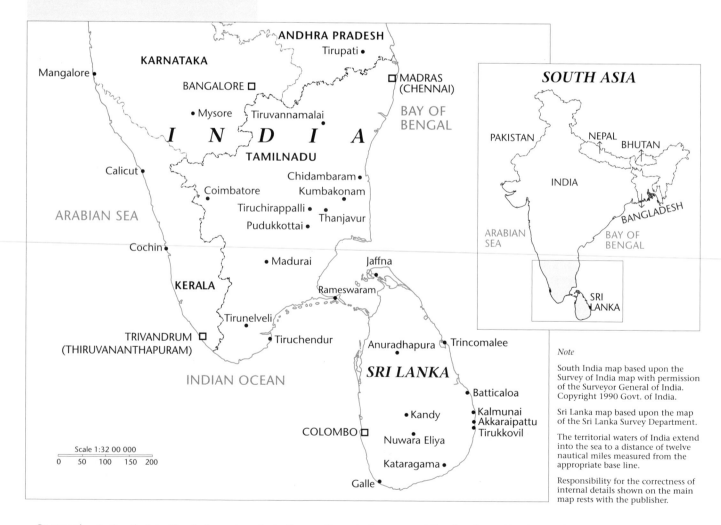

Note

South India map based upon the Survey of India map with permission of the Surveyor General of India. Copyright 1990 Govt. of India.

Sri Lanka map based upon the map of the Sri Lanka Survey Department.

The territorial waters of India extend into the sea to a distance of twelve nautical miles measured from the appropriate base line.

Responsibility for the correctness of internal details shown on the main map rests with the publisher.

Geography: In South Asia, Tamils live primarily in the southern Indian state of Tamilnadu and in the northern and eastern regions, as well as in the central highlands, of Sri Lanka. In addition to major towns and cities of the region, the approximate locations where photographs in this book were taken are also shown on the inset map.

SRI LANKA

The oldest Tamil settlements in Sri Lanka are located along the northern and eastern coasts. Fish from the semi-saline lagoons as well as coconuts augment the main food crop, rice.

Tamil labourers were imported from India in the late 19th and early 20th centuries to work on British tea estates in the Kandyan highlands of Sri Lanka. Exploited and denied citizenship after Independence in 1948, some "Estate Tamils" were repatriated to India in the 1960s and 1970s. Those who remained were finally given Sri Lankan citizenship in 1986.

The village of Panankadu, near Akkaraipattu, Amparai District, eastern Sri Lanka, is partially hidden under a dense growth of coconut, banana, and mango trees. Half of the Tamil-speaking people in this region are Hindus and the other half are Muslims.

Top
A mud and thatch house in Akkaraipattu, Amparai District. Tamil-speaking Hindus and Muslims in this region are matrilineal and matrilocal, providing a dowry house and some agricultural land for each of their daughters at marriage. Woven dried coconut fronds, which must be replaced every few years, are a cheap building material.

Above
A green sea of rice stretches across the irrigated coastal plain near Kalmunai, Amparai District. Larger landholdings and flat terrain in this region permit the use of tractors for cultivation. In the distance a crew of needy women is employed to weed the crop by hand.

Left
This is company housing on a tea plantation near Nuwara Eliya, Sri Lanka. Tamil women pick the tea leaves while the men work as pruners and tea processing workers. The building in the rear provides typical one-room quarters for Tamil labourer families, while the front building offers more spacious accommodation for foremen and supervisors.

Main street in Akkaraipattu, a Hindu and Muslim town of 40,000 in the eastern Tamil-speaking Batticaloa region. Most of the townsmen are farmers who commute to their rice fields daily. Shown as it appeared in the 1970s, Akkaraipattu has since suffered its share of violence and destruction as part of Sri Lanka's ethnic conflict.

CASTES AND OCCUPATIONS
Livelihood and social rank among Tamils is still strongly influenced by the Hindu caste system.

Although modern industrial and bureaucratic occupations are outside the framework of the caste system, work and social prestige in rural villages still conform to traditional expectations. Caste membership is hereditary, and people are expected to marry only members of their own subcaste. Although the system is hierarchical and exploitative, it traditionally provided, through patronage and reciprocal rights, a modest degree of economic security even to the lowest and most stigmatized groups. The English word "pariah" comes from the Tamil word *Paraiyar*, "Drummer," one of the so-called Untouchable castes.

Top left
Farmers and landowners are the economic and political foundation of the rural caste system. Tamil agricultural labourers are shown threshing rice beside the road near Madurai, Tamilnadu.

Top right
Fishermen provide an important food item for non-vegetarian families in South India and Sri Lanka. This Tamil man is hauling in his net for prawns in the Batticaloa lagoon, eastern Sri Lanka.

Centre
Washermen launder clothes and play an important role at life-crisis rituals such as births, weddings, and funerals. These Tamil washermen are beating clothes on washboard rocks near Akkaraipattu, Sri Lanka.

Bottom
Potters fashion everyday household cooking and water vessels. Every New Year, Tamil families buy new pots such as these for sale near Mayuram, Thanjavur District, Tamilnadu, to start the year afresh.

Left
Brassware and other articles of metal, wood, and stone are crafted by artisans of the Kammalar caste group. Here, a woman shops for new brass utensils in Tiruvannamalai, North Arcot District, Tamilnadu.

Right
Brahmins enjoy superior ritual status in the caste system. Two Brahman priests are shown opening a door at the famous Siva temple at Chidambaram, South Arcot District, Tamilnadu.

Left
Spinning and weaving are an important caste occupation as well as a major modern industry in India. This Tamil woman coils newly dyed cotton thread using an old bicycle wheel in Olappalayam, Coimbatore District, Tamilnadu.

Right
Untouchable drummers provide rhythms essential for funeral rites and for the conduct of ecstatic possession rituals associated with local Tamil Hindu goddesses. This Paraiyar caste man plays a *tampaṭṭam* drum in Kolavil Vadakku, near Akkaraipattu, eastern Sri Lanka.

SYMBOLIC HEAT

According to Hindu thought, at creation the original static and homogeneous life force devolved into opposing qualities and fluctuating states of being.

Our present universe now consists of constantly fluctuating situations, changing mixtures of many things, including the five primordial elements (*pūtams*), the three moral qualities (*guṇas*), and the three bodily humours (*muppiṇi*) – all of which are understood as manifestations of a deeper contrast and complementarity between male spirit and female substance (*purusha* and *prakriti*). In everyday life, efforts are constantly made to compensate for the changing forces and qualities which impinge upon the individual. Life, in short, is a balancing act.

Tamil beliefs about purity and gender are based upon Hindu concepts of a ranked universe.

Different species of beings – whether plants, animals, humans, or supernaturals – are viewed as unequal. One aspect of this ranking is a difference in degrees of religious status, sometimes permanent, as in the Brahman's priestly caste purity, and sometimes temporary, as in polluting life-cycle events (e.g., birth and death). Another crucial distinction is that of gender, the culturally prescribed ideas about male and female. According to Hindu theology, the cosmos is given form and consciousness by the male principle, but given energy and substance by the female principle. The male aspect of the universe is **passive and cool**, while the female aspect is **active and hot**. Tamils call it *Siva-Sakti*: the pairing of the male god *Siva*, who sustains the structure of the world, with his wife or female aspect *Sakti*, who provides the divine energy necessary to make things actually happen.

FOOD
Tamils in South India and Sri Lanka use ideas about hot/cold dualism in a practical way when they decide what to eat.

Most Tamils accept the idea that good health results from a balance of "heating" and "cooling" foods, i.e., foods which are thought to transmit internal states of heat and coolness to the body. These ideas of "symbolic heat" do *not* correspond exactly to Western scientific concepts of hot and cold: for example, in Sri Lanka, Tamils will say that a cup of hot tea is "cooling," while a cube of ice is "heating." The specific categorisation of heating and cooling foods varies a good deal from region to region, but the basic principle is widely accepted. In general, cow's milk and its by-products are cooling, as are many varieties of fruit. Many kinds of meat, on the other hand, as well as many pungent spices, such as garlic and chilli peppers, are heating. Classifications of heating and cooling foods are also found in Indonesia, in China, and in Latin America.

STATES OF MIND AND BODY
Ideas of "symbolic heat" also extend to beliefs about emotions and temporary conditions of the body.

The human body is known to be susceptible to changes in temperature, as in cases of fever, but Tamils also believe that heat is generated in the body by emotions (anger, erotic feelings), by certain bodily changes (menstruation, pregnancy), and by some divinely-caused illnesses (smallpox, skin eruptions). As a rule, states of temporary ritual pollution, such as those caused by menstruation or death, are associated with enhanced bodily heat. Any occupation, such as leatherworking or barbering, which brings one into contact with heating or polluting substances is believed to raise one's bodily heat. Temporary states of possession, in which a divine being is believed to enter one's body, are also considered "hot."

SEX AND GENDER
Some kinds of "symbolic heat" are permanently associated with females.

In the Hindu pantheon of gods, for example, male deities tend more often to be transcendant, passive, and "cool," while goddesses are usually more immanent, active, and "hot." The local-level goddesses worshipped in Tamil villages and urban neighbourhoods are typically "hot" and very significant in people's day-to-day lives, because they are believed capable of causing drought and disease. This broad pattern of male "coolness" and female "heat" is carried directly into ordinary thinking about men versus women. Anthropological fieldwork among Tamils in Sri Lanka revealed a general belief that women's bodies are "hotter" than those of men, and this was associated with the idea that women have more blood – an extremely "hot" substance – than men. Blood is understood as the source of bodily strength and power, so women are seen as the human embodiment of the cosmic female principle of energy, *sakti*.

COLOURS

White and red often symbolise the polarity of male and female, form and energy, stasis and change, coolness and heat.

A popular form of fortune-telling in south India involves blindly picking either red or white flowers. A white flower is regarded as "cool" and indicates "no change," but a red flower is considered "hot" and indicates "a change" is likely. Look for **white** and **red** as focal colours in body ornamentation, in life cycle ceremonies, and in Hindu religious symbolism throughout this book.

FOOD MEDICINE AND HEALTH

SYMBOLS AND SUBSTANCES
Symbols and substances are used to display group
identities and to transform internal states of the body.

In South Asia a person's identity is strongly linked to the social
categories of caste, ethnic group, and religious affiliation.
Anonymity or neutrality is not something most people want.
Instead, individuals often wear distinctive clothing and bodily
ornamentation, and observe explicit rules of diet and behaviour,
which set them apart as members of specific groups. These
symbolic marks of group identity are often created with the use of
colourful and aromatic substances, or with substances which
convey "heating" and "cooling" qualities.

A balanced diet means, for most Tamils, eating foods which do
not generate excessive heat or cold in the body.

Cosmetics, medicines, and spices have
overlapping uses and are sold in the same
shop here in Kumbakonam, Thanjavur
District, Tamilnadu. On the left are sacred
chalk sticks used to make the distinctive
"cooling" white Hindu forehead markings
(nāmam) which identify Vishnu devotees.
In the centre are dishes with shades of
kunkumam forehead pigment; red is the
traditional "hot" colour for fertile married
women, but nowadays a full range of
fashion colours is also available. On the
right is a pile of yellow turmeric root,
which is both a "cooling" spice for
cooking as well as a "cooling" cosmetic
for the skin. Orange coloured thread in
the rear may be worn to give supernatural
protection as well as providing an
inexpensive way to tie the Tamil wedding
emblem, the tāli, around a bride's neck.

Above

The "cooling" margosa tree, *Azadirachta indica,* is called *vēppamaram* in Tamil and *neem* in north India. Its leaves, its sap, and the oil pressed from its fruit, although extremely bitter, are believed to have profoundly "cooling" powers when used medicinally or in the Hindu worship of "hot" deities. Several popular modern brands of "cooling" bath soap are manufactured which contain margosa to help cure heat-caused pimples and skin conditions. This photo was taken near Batticaloa, Sri Lanka.

Left

Grinding spices for cooking is a daily activity in Tamil kitchens. Here a housewife in Akkaraipattu, Sri Lanka, uses a grinding stone to make a curry paste containing garlic and dried red chillies (both "heating") along with yellow turmeric powder and some freshly grated coconut (both "cooling"). Curry itself is not a spice. This Tamil word *(kari)* refers to any combination of spices and other ingredients used to make the sauces ("curries") which are eaten with rice.

Opposite page

Marks of a Hindu religious sect are painted on the face of a Tamil man, using chalk from a sacred quarry. The squared shape of the *nāmam* design on his forehead indicates that he belongs specifically to the "southern" *(teṅkalai)* sect of Vishnu worshippers. The white chalk and the yellow sandalwood paste are masculine and "cooling" while the red pigment is feminine and "heating." Overall, the mark reflects a cosmic balance of male and female, but it is also true that the male element dominates and contains the female. This man is a non-Brahmin attendant at the Srirangam temple, near Tiruchirapalli, Tamilnadu.

Vegetarian dishes offered annually to the spirits of the dead are set out on the floor before guests are invited to share them, as shown in this photo from Akkaraipattu, Sri Lanka. Vegetables and dairy products are generally less "heating" than meat, as well as ethically superior on the grounds of *ahimsā,* the Hindu-Jain doctrine of non-violence. While only a minority of Hindus are strict vegetarians, most will at least observe vegetarian vows during special religious events. Dishes shown include (clockwise from upper left) deep fried *palakāram* sweets, fruits (banana and jak), yoghurt, more fried and steamed sweets, vegetable curries, more yoghurt, *kānci* rice gruel, fried green plantain, *sothi* coconut milk gravy, several more vegetable curries (both wet and dry), and green-skinned oranges and mangoes.

A non-vegetarian restaurant in Madras (Chennai) advertises itself as a "Hindu military hotel." The word "hotel" is widely used in South Asia to mean restaurant. The word "military" refers to the non-vegetarian diet of kings and warriors, who proudly eat meat for the "heat" and "energy" *(sakti)* it supplies. Finally, the word "Hindu" assures patrons that the management and kitchen staff are neither Muslims nor Christians, so no beef will be served on the premises.

STAPLES OF THE DIET
Vegetables, grains, fruits, and spices may convey "heating" or "cooling" properties.

Rice and lentils are the foundation of the diet in South India and Sri Lanka. Both Hindu and Buddhist religious pictures are also sold in this grain shop at the island-wide pilgrimage centre of Kataragama, Sri Lanka.

Top
Vegetables of many kinds used in Indian and Sri Lankan cooking are seen for sale at a roadside stall at Tissamaharama, near Kataragama, in southern Sri Lanka.

Bottom
Chillies and bananas represent two poles of the hot/cold food continuum, shown here for sale in Colombo, Sri Lanka. Dried red chillies are "heating" while bananas are "cooling." The Sinhalese Buddhists as well as the Tamils in Sri Lanka follow a system of hot/cold dietary rules.

Top
Deep-fried snacks made with chickpeas, lentils, and spices, are often considered "heating," although some snacks soaked in yogurt are "cooling." Here a sidewalk entrepreneur sells different types of *vaḍai* and *boṇḍa* snacks in Tiruchirappalli, Tamilnadu.

Bottom
Coffee and tea, heavily sweetened and often mixed with milk, provide popular roadside refreshments. In eastern Sri Lanka, Tamils say that tea is "cooling" and should be taken during the heat of the day, while coffee is "heating" and should be taken in the cool of the evening. In South India, however, coffee is consumed at all hours. This vendor dramatically pours a cup of coffee in Olappalaiyam, Coimbatore District, Tamilnadu.

FAST FOODS
Even sidewalk snacks and beverages convey "heating" and "cooling" properties when consumed.

MEDICINE AND CURING

Ayurvedic medical theories seek an equilibrium of three bodily humours: bile (a source of heat), wind (a source of motion), and phlegm (a cooling aqueous connection).

Āyurvēda, the "science of longevity," is an ancient Hindu school of medicine with many modern practitioners today. Ayurvedic specialists prescribe both diet and herbal medicines to restore an internal balance of humours within the body. Diagnosis and treatment can be very complex in Ayurveda, but the simpler everyday Tamil concepts of "heating" versus "cooling" foods reflect some of the basic ideas of Ayurveda.

Many systems of curing coexist with Ayurvedic medicine. Patients may resort to astrology, religious pilgrimage, or Western antibiotics, depending on their pragmatic results.

Following page
An Ayurvedic physician in Tambiluvil, eastern Sri Lanka, examines his stock of medicinal oils and herbal remedies. In addition to printed medical books (upper left), there are older texts called *ēḍu*, inscribed with a stylus onto dried palmyra palm leaves and strung together with cord (upper right).

Left
A pot of holy water is prepared by the priest of the Pattirakali Temple in Akkaraipattu, eastern Sri Lanka. Charged with the power of *mantras* (verbal spells), the water will be sprinkled on the woman to guard against minor demons who seek to trouble her.

Right
A fertility problem brings Tamil women to make an offering to stone images of the cobra deity flanking the *lingam* at this outdoor shrine to the god Siva at Tiruvannamalai, North Arcot District, Tamilnadu. "Cooling" yellow turmeric and sandalwood paste have been smeared on the stone icons to obtain a blessing.

GENDER AND THE LIFE CYCLE

CHILDHOOD AND EDUCATION
Growing up is marked by a series of initiations. Physical growth, secular education, and spiritual development are seen as interrelated.

Although only the most orthodox Hindus perform all of them, the life cycle rites (*samskāras*) begin with rituals for conception and safe pregnancy; continue through rituals of naming, tonsure, first feeding, beginning of education, religious initiation, and marriage; and conclude with mortuary and ancestral rites.

A small boy carries lunch cannisters to his mother while she works on repairs to the steps surrounding the bathing tank at the Meenakshi Sundaresvarar Temple in Madurai, Tamilnadu. At this age, children are cherished for their innocence and purity of heart.

Students honour Sarasvati, the goddess of learning, by following her image in procession each year at the Tamil high school in Akkaraipattu, eastern Sri Lanka. White clothing and flowers symbolise purity and spirituality; skirts rather than saris symbolise a stage of life prior to full womanhood.

Learning is a ritual process.

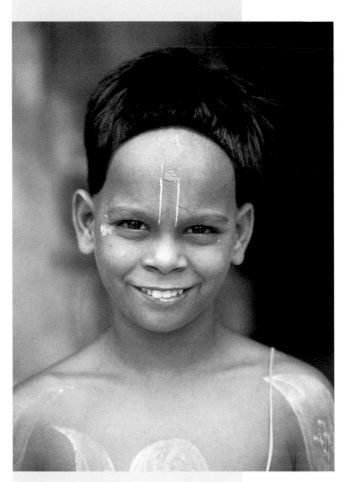

Left
A Brahmin boy wears marks of religious initiation at the Srirangam Temple near Tiruchirappalli, Tamilnadu. The shaven forehead and sacred thread are symbolic of a Brahmin's "twice born" status.

Right
The start of formal education is an initiation ritual for Tamil first-graders at a school in Akkaraipattu, Sri Lanka. The Hindu priest hands out palm leaves inscribed with letters from the Tamil alphabet, after which each child traces the letters with a finger in a tray of rice. The Tamil alphabet has 246 original letters, plus 65 more "northern letters" considered politically incorrect nowadays by pro-Dravidian scholars, which were borrowed from Sanskrit, an ancient Indo-Aryan language.

FEMALE PUBERTY

Tamil families joyfully celebrate their daughters' coming of age. Rituals of first menstruation treat the girl as if she were a bride.

Tamils in eastern Sri Lanka believe that blood is central to human growth and maturation: blood is the "refined" product of digestion which is then further "refined" into muscle, bone, and *both* male and female semen. The onset of menstruation and of sexual feeling during adolescence is traditionally considered to be the hydraulic result of excess blood production and a consequence of the hot, energetic properties of blood itself. Women are believed to be naturally endowed with more blood, thus have more raw energy (*sakti*), than men, but menstruation regularly drains off some of this potential. Excess blood is "refined" into semen, which is stored in the brain. With celibacy and asceticism, this concentrated and solidified sexual essence can be transmuted into mental and spiritual power.

A girl's first menstruation has a paradoxical value: at the outset the power manifest in her body is considered to be highly polluting, so she is immediately put into seclusion. Her body is said to be very "hot," so she is fed "cooling" foods and substances, such as margosa oil. Yet an astrologer will also use the exact time of her first menstrual stain to calculate a new horoscope of her future. As her state of pollution diminishes over nearly a week, the child is made ready to re-emerge as a woman. For the gala celebration on the final day, formal printed invitations may have been distributed, and the house will have been decorated with cloths and auspicious brass pots. Near the well, several auspicious women (*sumaṅkalis*, all married and having children) pour water over the girl to remove the last bit of pollution.

For the first time in public the girl wears a sari, often in wedding colours of pink or red, and she is ritually honoured by the women as if she were a bride. In Tamil culture, a wedding (*kaliyāṇam*) is the epitome of joy and auspiciousness, so by analogy this event is sometimes called in Tamil a "puberty wedding." She then steps across the threshold into her house as a new woman and sits with a young female cousin on a special bridal throne to receive gifts and best wishes from her relatives, friends, and neighbours. In parts of Tamilnadu, the mock-wedding idea is carried to the point of actually dressing the young female cousin in male clothes as a "groom." All of these puberty rituals are conducted largely by women, in contrast to the male priests generally required in most Hindu rituals.

Tamils celebrate a "wedding" when their daughters first come of age. The event dramatises her eligibility for a real wedding later on.

The threshold is a symbolic focus for this "rite of passage," for it is through this doorway that the girl re-enters society after her transformation into a woman. These rituals closely follow the stages of separation, liminality, and reincorporation first postulated for all "rites of passage" by Arnold Van Gennep in his classic sociological work of 1909.

Opposite page
The final bath prepares the girl for her puberty celebration in Akkaraipattu, Sri Lanka. A *sumaṅkali*, an "auspicious" woman having husband and children, must pour the water to remove any lingering menstrual pollution. Inside the temporary bathing enclosure, this girl stands on a broom to deter any lurking spirits.

Left
Dressed as a bride, this girl in Tambiluvil, near Tirukkovil, Sri Lanka, is ritually honoured and worshipped with lighted tapers outside the threshold of her house. She wears a sari for the first time in public, often one of pink or red, the favoured colour for a bride. In her hand she holds a decorated *kumbam* pot, an icon of the divine which is symbolic of her own sacredness and her future prosperity.

Seated on a wedding throne inside her house in Akkaraipattu, Sri Lanka, a puberty girl receives gifts and congratulations from her invited guests. Seated beside her is her "companion girl," *tōḻippeṇ*, a female cousin who serves to detract the evil eye, and standing nearby is her very proud younger brother.

In eastern Sri Lanka, where the post-marital residence pattern is matrilocal, a girl's "puberty house" eventually becomes her own dowry and marriage house. The doorway of this dwelling in Akkaraipattu, Sri Lanka, is adorned with customary numbers of cloths and brass pots, which are special marks of matrilineal clan honour in this region. On the table are additional decorative items, including a new radio.

In this picture from Akkaraipattu, eastern Sri Lanka, the groom prepares to tie a gold necklace holding the marriage symbol, a small gold amulet called the *tāli*, around the bride's neck. Red or pink is the most common colour for bridal saris, while grooms usually wear white. Red is also the traditional colour for the forehead mark (*poṭṭu*) of Tamil wives during the childbearing years. As if to temper the "hot" erotic impulses associated with marriage, the bridal couple are served a "cooling" mixture of fruit and milk. In Hindu thought, marriage is believed to be necessary to channel and control a woman's innate cosmic energy; therefore an unmarried woman – or goddess – is potentially dangerous. Kinship systems in Tamilnadu and Sri Lanka encourage marriage with a cross-cousin (i.e., one's mother's brother's child or one's father's sister's child), and marriage between a man and his elder sister's daughter is also sanctioned in parts of Tamilnadu.

MARRIAGE & GENDER

Tamil weddings express male/female gender symbolism through colour. The groom wears "cool" white and the bride wears red, the "hottest" colour.

The colour of everyday clothing also reflects gender symbolism. Men prefer white, which is "cool" and austere, while women, especially during their childbearing years, indulge in vivid colours associated with activity and fecundity.

White turbans, shirt, and *vēṭṭi* waistcloth are typical attire for Tamil cultivators. Here two men enjoy a shady rest beside the road in Olappalaiyam, Coimbatore District, Tamilnadu.

Following page
Coloured saris and blouses worn by Tamil women stand out, particularly at festive events. These women are husking rice with mortar and pestle for a ritual at the Pattirakali Temple in Akkaraipattu, Sri Lanka.

WOMEN PREFER COLOURS

Left
A Muslim wife in blue from Akkaraipattu, Sri Lanka, covers her head with the end of her sari in deference to Islamic ideals of female modesty. Despite the difference in religion, these Tamil-speaking Muslims share with the Hindus many cultural assumptions about cold and hot, male and female. Carrying a child is also an informal way for women, both Muslim and Hindu, to safeguard their reputation in public.

Right
A Hindu college student home on vacation in Akkaraipattu, Sri Lanka, posed for this picture in one of her "hottest" and most colourful saris. A girl's family will often use photographs such as this to help find a suitable marriage partner for her.

MEN PREFER WHITE

Top
A Muslim merchant in Akkaraipattu,
Sri Lanka, wears a Western-style shirt and
traditional *sarong*, both white. The Tamil-
speaking Muslims of Sri Lanka are
sometimes called Moors, a name given
them by the Portuguese in the 16th
century.

Right
Two Tamil professionals wet their feet
in the sea to obtain a sacred blessing
from Lord Murugan. White clothing is
particularly important for men visiting
Hindu holy places, such as here at
Tiruchendur, Tirunelveli District,
Tamilnadu.

ASCETICISM AND OLD AGE

Heat is generated by asceticism and meditation. Some older men may enter a state of world-renunciation, even become religious mendicants, but Tamils of all ages make ascetic vows of pilgrimage and personal devotion.

In Hinduism, the person who can discharge his worldly duties and thereafter renounce the pleasures and temptations of mortal existence may become a *sādhu* or *sanniyāsi*. The performance of ascetic penances is believed to generate power in the form of spiritual heat, *tapas*, which is stored in the body of the renouncer. Hindu mythology records examples of how this power of ascetic heat even compels the gods to obey. Relatively few men become full-fledged *sanniyāsis*, but many, like this man in Tirukkovil, Sri Lanka, become more involved with Hindu devotional practices in their old age.

Religious asceticism is a strong element in Tamil culture.

Top

Tamil pilgrims walk to Kataragama every year to fulfill personal vows. These men set out from homes in Jaffna, at the extreme northern tip of Sri Lanka, to walk 300 miles south to Kataragama, in the southeastern corner of the island. There both Tamil Hindus and Sinhalese Buddhists jointly worship the god Kataragama, known also to Tamils as Murugan. Military blockades in Sri Lanka's ethnic conflict have prevented this pilgrimage from happening in recent years. This photo was taken along the east coast road near Akkaraipattu, Sri Lanka.

Bottom

Three *sanniyāsi* holy men, sit inside the temple at Tiruvannamalai, North Arcot District, Tamilnadu, soliciting alms from charitable worshippers. The garments of Hindu holy men are traditionally dyed with ochre, a red mineral pigment which also suggests their inner ascetic "heat."

HINDU WORSHIP

TEMPLES AND ICONS

Although ultimately the soul and the universe are one, to ordinary Hindus the focus of worship is a complex hierarchy of gods. Local village goddesses embody "heat" which can harm or heal.

Hindu scriptures teach the ultimate unity of soul and cosmos, but ordinary mortals can be led to that realisation only through more concrete devotional practices. In their daily lives most Tamils seek the practical protection and blessings of Hindu gods through formal acts of worship, called *pūja*. Gods are called into stone or metal images housed in temples, which may be sumptuous or simple. The great medieval temples of Tamilnadu are impressive monuments to the belief that the loftiest gods must be housed in palaces and entertained like divine sovereigns. However, in the Tamil countryside and in urban neighbourhoods, local deities – particularly temperamental, "hot," and potentially angry goddesses – are considered more important to health and prosperity.

White and red temple walls symbolise the balance of form and energy, male and female, *Siva and Sakti*. The foundation myths of many temples in Tamilnadu also reveal that eventsinvolving milk and blood are symbolically associated with the establishment of their sanctity. Here a bullock-cart rounds the massive stone walls of the Vishnu temple in Tirukurunkudi, Tirunelveli District, Tamilnadu.

The contrast of male and female is emphasised in Hindu worship.

Hindu temples reached their greatest architectural development in South India. As a consequence of the Tamil diaspora, new temples based on these same ancient designs are now being constructed in Europe and North America.

Opposite page
A red village goddess displays the marks of her ambivalent personality. Her crimson colour connotes "heat" and anger, and her fangs confirm her ferocious temperament. However, she holds two children in her arms, indicating that she is also a mother capable of using her ferocity to protect those she loves. Most Tamil village goddesses are addressed as "mother," *amman*. If angered they can cause drought and skin diseases associated with "heat," such as smallpox. If worshipped and propitiated they will provide rains and good health for members of the local community. This picture is from Rameswaram Island, Ramanathapuram District, Tamilnadu.

Top
A row of stone *lingams* represents Siva, a male deity of transcendent importance to Hindus, in this photo from Kumbakonam, Thanjavur District, Tamilnadu. The vertical "male" column is embedded in a circular "female" slab, forming a stylised representation of cosmic union. The *lingam* is customarily washed with "cooling" substances such as coconut water, yogurt, and clarified butter, then anointed with fragrant sandalwood paste, before worship.

Bottom
A row of local "hot" goddesses, each represented by a small metal face, has been temporarily erected for an annual festival. Although they may lack a permanent temple building, such local goddesses nevertheless receive tremendous devotion at special times of the year. Here at a small hamlet west of Kokkatticcolai, Batticaloa District, Sri Lanka, several goddesses have been given "cooling" offerings of fruit, coconut flower, and margosa leaves.

Left

The great temples of Tamilnadu are centres of sociability and commerce as well as of worship. Their massive stone construction keeps them cool in the heat of the day, and many people come to rest and to shop from nearby merchants. The western gateway tower, or *gōpuram*, looms over women relaxing inside the walls of the famous temple at Tiruvannamalai, North Arcot District, Tamilnadu.

Right

A close-up view of a *gōpuram* tower at the Meenakshi Sundaresvarar Temple in Madurai, Tamilnadu, suggests the richness and complexity of Hindu mythology and iconography, as well as the lavishness of royal patronage. Towers erected at the cardinal directions, each with its own gateway, give access through massive stone walls to the inner shrines of the temple.

The new Venkatesvarar Temple in
Pittsburgh, PA, linked to the wealthy
Vishnu temple at Tirupati, Andhra
Pradesh, was built with a combination of
traditional South Indian craftsmanship
and modern architectural engineering.

WORSHIP

Hindu worship takes many forms in South India and Sri Lanka. Because sacredness itself generates heat, worshippers seek to cool and calm the deity.

Tamils, like most Hindus, regard sacredness as a force field. When gods are present, and particularly when they grant an opportunity to be viewed (*darshan*), their power pervades the space nearby. Under amplified conditions of ritual, some gods exert enough influence to enter human bodies, causing temporary states of trance possession. The general strategy of Hindu worship is to honour and please the deity and thereby to gain blessings and boons. The most elaborate forms of worship (*pūja*) involve offerings of food, fragrant aromas, gleaming lights, musical sounds, emblems of power, and recitations of praise. In addition, gods are periodically carried in procession from the temple to survey their domain and to transmit their protective blessings to individual households.

The Tamils honour and entertain their gods in processions.

Opposite page
Water-filled pots embody the "hot" goddess Mariyamman in a street procession in an artisan caste (*Kammāḷar*) neighbourhood in Kumbakonam, Thanjavur District, Tamilnadu. As the young boys carry the sacred *kumbam* pots, the "heat" generated in their bodies by such direct contact with the sacred is "cooled" with water sprinkled over their bodies by friendly bystanders. Notice the "cooling" turmeric on top as well as the "cooling" margosa leaves which serve as an insulation layer between the pots and the boys' heads.

Bottom
A shoulder-borne palanquin is the traditional way to take the god Pillaiyar (Ganesh) in an evening procession around his temple in Karaitivu, near Kalmunai, Sri Lanka. A yak-tail whisk is waved before the god as a mark of respect, and the privileged bearers have removed their shirts as a further gesture of devotion.

New technology is adapted to sacred purposes when a Massey-Ferguson tractor is employed to transport the god Pillaiyar (Ganesh) in a daytime procession to the beach. Note, too, the portable loudspeakers which help to propagate Pillaiyar's blessings as his procession moves through the market area of Akkaraipattu, Sri Lanka.

SACRED FOOD

Food for the gods is usually vegetarian and "cooling," but not always. Some fierce deities demand meat and intoxicants.

Gods eat before humans, but they only consume the subtle essence of the food placed before them. What remains, in a sense, is the divine leftovers. Worshippers, grateful to receive anything blessed by the god's table, receive shares of the returned offering, called *prasadam*. In this picture from Akkaraipattu, Sri Lanka, a "cooling" vegetarian meal of rice, vegetable curry, yogurt, sweets, and fruit has been served to a Tamil household goddess.

Following page
Sweetened milk-rice is a popular offering to Hindu gods. Called *poṅkal* or *pukkai*, it is also cooked to celebrate the Tamil new year holiday of Tai Pongal in January-February. Cow's milk is an ingredient which contributes to its "coolness." At dawn on the morning of Tai Pongal, as an auspicious sign of prosperity to come, this Tamil woman in Akkaraipattu, Sri Lanka, waits for the milk to boil over the side of the pot before she adds the rice.

Tamil homes are centres of ritual and religious activity.

Left
A professional priest is not always necessary for domestic rituals. Here an experienced older layman serves boiled rice for a household goddess, represented by a water-filled brass pot and coconut, in Akkaraipattu, Sri Lanka. Banana leaves are used only once, then discarded, like paper plates

Top
Tamil Hindu homes always have a shrine of some kind. In eastern Sri Lanka the shrine is usually located at the centre of the house, in a secure windowless room which is also used to store rice and valuables. The shrine room in this Tamil house in Akkaraipattu, Sri Lanka, has been decorated for a special *pūja* to the household goddess, whose metal face is decorated with both red ("hot") and white ("cool") flowers. On the rear wall are inexpensive pictures of other popular Hindu gods.

FIREWALKING AND POSSESSION

Local goddesses are vivid embodiments of divine energy for many Tamils. Firewalking rituals conjoin actual fire with "symbolic heat" to celebrate the power of the goddess.

Right
Turmeric paste and margosa leaves "cool" a devotee who has vowed to walk the bed of coals for a local goddess. Such vows are usually a contractual repayment for divine help with some practical problem, such as a sick child or a lost cow. He wears a protective cotton string around his neck during a period of religious austerities before the annual firewalking at the Draupadi Amman Temple in Pandiruppu, near Kalmunai, Sri Lanka.

Opposite page
Animals may be sacrificed to the more ferocious deities at the annual temple festivals. Even liquor and marijuana may be offered if a deity is traditionally known to expect it. At the Pattirakali temple in Akkaraipattu, Sri Lanka, a partially paralyzed man is being held by assistants while the spirit suspected of causing his malady is urged to leave his body in exchange for the immediate sacrifice of a white rooster. A coconut is also chopped in half to "cut" any magical spells impeding the man's recovery. Such curing methods sometimes seem to work, although unfortunately not in this particular case.

Pattirakali receives both "hot" and "cool" offerings which reflect her ambivalent character as a ferocious, yet protective, goddess.

Fire-walking is the climax of many goddess festivals in eastern Sri Lanka.

Top
Rice cooked with "cooling" yellow turmeric is wrapped in banana leaves and served to the goddess Pattirakali each year in Akkaraipattu, Sri Lanka.

Bottom
A white rooster is promised as an offering to the goddess Pattirakali. The goddess, speaking through the man crouching in trance, has selected this particular bird to be sacrificed first. Although a blood sacrifice is extremely "heating," the goddess demands it once each year, after which she is placated and her anger is "cooled." The initial birds to be sacrificed are "cooling" white in colour.

Top
A pit of long-burning hardwood is ignited with elaborate rituals about eight hours before the firewalking, as shown in this photo from Akkaraipattu, Sri Lanka.

Centre
The coals are carefully fanned and tamped to ensure a solid bed for walking, while a large crowd of onlookers assembles at a Pattirakali temple in Karaitivu, near Kalmunai, Sri Lanka.

Bottom
At the signal, a line of devotees crosses the fire holding "cooling" margosa leaves. The third man carries his son, fulfilling in literal fashion a vow that his boy will "cross the fire" to repay the goddess' favour.

The goddess is said to protect the feet of her devotees by laying down the invisible end of her sari over the coals. A small number receive burns, which are attributed to a lack of faith. For most participants, the firewalking is a reaffirmation of the the goddess' power to control heat and to protect her steadfast devotees from harm. This turmeric-coated man clutches margosa leaves as he crosses a pit of hot coals at the Draupadi Amman temple in Pandiruppu, near Kalmunai, Sri Lanka.

SUGGESTIONS FOR FURTHER READING

THE TAMILS

E. Valentine Daniel,
Fluid Signs: Being a Person the Tamil Way.
University of California Press 1984.

Nicholas Dirks,
The Hollow Crown: Ethnohistory of an Indian Kingdom.
Cambridge University Press 1987.

Gabriella Eichinger Ferro-Luzzi,
Cool Fire: Culture-Specific Themes in Tamil Short Stories.
Gottingen: Edition Herodot 1983.

Oddvar Hollup,
Bonded Labour: Caste and Cultural Identity Among Tamil Plantation Workers in Sri Lanka.
New Delhi: Sterling 1994.

Karin Kapadia,
Siva and Her Sisters:
Gender, Caste, and Class in Rural South India.
Boulder, CO: Westview 1995.

Dennis B. McGilvray, ed.,
Caste Ideology and Interaction.
Cambridge University Press 1982.

Michael Moffatt,
An Untouchable Community in South India:
Structure and Consensus.
Princeton University Press 1979.

Bryan Pfaffenberger,
Caste in Tamil Culture: The Religious Foundations of Sudra Domination in Tamil Sri Lanka.
Foreign & Comparative Studies, South Asian Series 7.
Syracuse University 1982.

A.K. Ramanujan, trans.
Poems of Love and War: From the Eight Anthologies and the Ten Long Poems of Classical Tamil.
Columbia University Press 1985.

Stanley J. Tambiah,
Sri Lanka: Ethnic Fratricide and the Dismantling of Democracy.
University of Chicago Press 1986.

SYMBOLIC HEAT: FOOD, MEDICINE, AND HEALTH

Brenda E.F. Beck,
"Colour and heat in South Indian ritual."
Man 4:553-72, December 1972.

Gabriella Eichinger Ferro-Luzzi,
"Food avoidance at puberty and during menstruation in Tamilnad."
Ecology of Food and Nutrition 2:1-8, 1973

Srinivasa B. Mani,
"From marriage to child conception: an ethnomedical study in rural Tamilnadu," in Giri Raj Gupta, ed.,
The Social and Cultural Context of Medicine in India.
New Delhi: Vikas 1981.

Dennis B. McGilvray,
"Sexual power and fertility in Sri Lanka: Batticaloa Tamils and Moors," in Carol P. MacCormack, ed.,
Ethnography of Fertility and Birth.
Academic Press 1982.
(2nd edition, Waveland Press, 1994).

Mark and Mimi Nichter, eds.
Anthropology and International Health:
Asian Case Studies.
Amsterdam: Gordon and Breach 1996.

Gananath Obeyesekere,
"The impact of Ayurvedic ideas on the culture and the individual in Sri Lanka," in Charles Leslie, ed.,
Asian Medical Systems: A Comparative Study.
University of California Press 1976.

GENDER AND THE LIFE CYCLE

Richard L. Brubaker,
"Lustful woman, chaste wife, ambivalent goddess:
a South Indian myth."
Anima 3:59-62, 1977.

Margaret Trawick,
Notes on Love in a Tamil Family.
University of California Press 1990.

George L. Hart, III.,
"Women and the sacred in Ancient Tamilnad."
Journal of Asian Studies 32:233-50, February 1973.

Dennis B. McGilvray,
"Households in Akkaraipattu: dowry and domestic
organization among the matrilineal Tamils and Moors
of Sri Lanka" in John Gray & David Mearns, eds.,
*Society from the Inside Out: Anthropological Perspectives
on the South Asian Household.*
Sage Publications 1989.

Kalpana Ram,
*Mukkuvar Women: Gender, Hegemony, and Capitalist
Transformation in a South Indian Fishing Community.*
London & New Jersey: Zed Books 1991.

Arnold Van Gennep,
The Rites of Passage. Paris: E. Nourry 1909.
English edition,
University of Chicago Press 1960.

Susan S. Wadley, ed.,
The Powers of Tamil Women.
Foreign & Comparative Studies,
South Asian Series 6. Syracuse University 1980.

Anthony Good,
*The Female Bridegroom: A Comparative Study of
Life-Crisis Rituals in South India and Sri Lanka.*
Oxford: Clarendon Press 1991.

Deborah Winslow
"Rituals of First Menstruation in Sri Lanka."
Man 15(4): 603-625, December 1980.

HINDU WORSHIP

Lawrence A. Babb,
*The Divine Hierarchy:
Popular Hinduism in Central India.*
Columbia University Press 1975.

Gabriella Eichinger Ferro-Luzzi,
"The logic of South Indian food offerings."
Anthropos 72:529-56, 1977.

C.J. Fuller,
*The Camphor Flame:
Popular Hinduism and Society in India.*
Princeton University Press 1992.

Patricia Lawrence,
"The Changing Amman: Notes on the Injury of War in
Eastern Sri Lanka."
South Asia 20, Special Issue 1997.

Dennis B. McGilvray,
"The 1987 Sterling Award Essay:
Sex, Repression and Sanskritization in Sri Lanka?"
Ethos 16:99-127, June 1988.

Manuel Moreno & McKim Marriott,
"Humoral transactions in two Tamil cults:
Murukan and Mariyamman."
in McKim Marriott, ed.,
India Through Hindu Categories.
Sage Publications 1990.

Wendy O'Flaherty,
Asceticism and Eroticism in the Mythology of Siva.
Oxford University Press 1973.

David Dean Shulman,
*Tamil Temple Myths: Sacrifice and Divine Marriage in the
South Indian Saiva Tradition.*
Princeton University Press 1980.